To You Do Greatness

—

A Parable On Success *And* Significance

Rick E. Amidon

Rex M. Rogers

© 2011 by Rick E. Amidon and Rex M. Rogers

Published by Unlikely Leaders, LLC

unlikelyleaders@gmail.com

Print publication in the United States of America.

ISBN   978-0-9837693-2-3

"God is in heaven and you are on earth,

so let your words be few."

Ecclesiastes 5:3

Rex Rogers

Micah 6:8

Preface

This is a book about greatness, leadership, faith, and ultimately, life itself. It's a short story about an immigrant named Danu whose memories include a loving father who encouraged him to "do greatness."

In Danu's story you'll find experiences and choices similar to those you face in your own life. Danu obtains an education, finds a profession, works diligently, and matures. He does "his thing" based largely upon the philosophy of life—assumptions, values, perspectives, and attitudes—he inherited from his family and culture.

Like Danu, all of us possess a philosophy of life, whether recognized or unrecognized, well considered or unexamined. Our philosophy of life forms the bedrock of who we are, what values we embrace, what choices we make, and, therefore, who we become.

Alongside Danu's life story in this book you'll find another point of view. It's an annotation of Danu's values and choices based upon a Christian worldview—a philosophy of life grounded in God's word, the Bible. These sections will enable you to re-examine Danu's values and choices using a Christian worldview as your lens. What you see may surprise you.

We encourage you to overlay Danu's story with your own. You will learn as Danu learns, so that you, too, will be able to do greatness.

Rick E. Amidon, Ph.D.
Founder, mark217
Former President,
Baker College of Muskegon
and Sanford-Brown College

Rex M. Rogers, Ph.D.
President, SAT-7 USA
Former President,
Cornerstone University

Today You Do Greatness

This is a story about Danu.

And leadership.

And providence.

But mostly it's a story about greatness.

True greatness.

What it is.

And how you do it.

How many things do you attempt,

daily,

which result in

your

greatness?

True excellence.

Greatness which leads you to peace.

To joy,

      so different than its orphaned half-brother,

      happiness.

Greatness

Most people at some point in their lives fantasize about greatness. Many people take it to the next level and actually aspire to greatness, and a few make genuine attempts to achieve it. What would it be like to be elected President of the United States? Wouldn't it be great to gain fame as a social reformer like Rosa Parks, or to be considered the epitome of compassion like Mother Teresa? Or maybe you'd like to be the world's greatest athlete— like Muhammad Ali, Michael Jordan, or Annika Sorenstam—renowned for your competitive prowess and skill in some favorite sport. Or perhaps in your fantasies, greatness is equated with financial success or net worth. Well, than who is greater? Oprah Winfrey or Donald Trump or Bill Gates or Queen Elizabeth?

Dreaming about greatness is pretty common stuff. We've all done it. We all do it. From the business executive to the soloist, from the researcher to the kid playing ball in the park, dreaming we'll be the greatest is as much a part of life as breathing. It comes from something inside us, a sense that what's before us is not all there is, a desire for something more or deeper.

Aspiring to greatness can be selfishly driven, as in a Nixon-like quest for power and control. It can be selflessly driven, as in St. Francis of Assisi's, "Preach the Word at all times; when necessary, use words." It can be other-centered, as in a mother's hope for her child.

Our dreams of greatness are rooted in an intrinsic desire for meaning, for significance, for doing something that matters. Our humanity makes us want to be somebody. We want to do something that lasts, something that makes our mortal selves immortal.

Danu often asked himself,

"Why greatness?"

What is there about greatness

That makes it

Strangely agreeable

To all people in all nations

At all times?

Why Greatness

In the Bible God tells us the "why" and "for what" of our lives should be about obedience of his moral will, service in his calling, and excellence in our works. In this divine scenario greatness is possible. Greatness is always providential though not always predictable. Greatness is, rightly grounded, a blessing, a gift to be used for good, an outcome more than a goal.

The Bible never identifies greatness as a goal unto itself. Jesus asked his disciples, "Who is greater, the one who is at the table or the one who serves?" (Luke 22:24-27). His answer was "the one who is at the table," speaking from the world's perspective. Yet then he said, "but I am among you as one who serves," reminding us that God blesses those who love and give.

Greatness is a rare disposition that is always a by-product of obedience, service, and excellence. The word "greatness" is used more than twenty times in the Old Testament book of Nehemiah, referring to a great trouble, great call, great opportunity, great compassion, great Lord, or great joy, but never a great man. Nehemiah did a great work for a great God. The prophet Micah says it this way, "What does the Lord require of you? To act justly, to love mercy, and to walk humbly with your God" (6:8).

Obedience determines whether our actions are in accordance with our Creator's definition of reality. Service determines whether our activities are noble or ignoble. Excellence determines whether our work attains a level worthy of appreciation or admiration.

The New Testament book of Colossians says "Whatever you do, work at it with all your heart, as working for the Lord, not for men" (3:23).

Our values show through our work. If we do shoddy work, we're saying that the service or product does not matter, that those who use the service or product do not matter, and that there is no one to whom we are accountable for our activity. It's meaningless.

On the contrary, when God is there, work is meaningful.

Danu is from India.

His mentor is his father, Godeep.

Godeep.

A name reflecting both intention

and purpose.

Godeep's influence over Danu

was immense.

Though his family raised him to be a good man,

Danu had his eyes on more.

And it was Godeep who taught Danu

to aspire to greatness.

Greatness, to Godeep, meant being highly

accomplished,

effective in achieving goals, and

attaining renown.

God Is Great

We want to "be great" because our Creator is great.

The Word of God, the Bible, does not contain a passage commending "greatness" like the verses describing love in 1 Corinthians 13. But there are great people in the Bible. Deborah was a great judge, even though her culture emphasized her place as a woman-in-a-man's-world. David, the flawed shepherd king, achieved greatness as the "man after God's own heart." Nehemiah was great, yet he was but the king's cupbearer.

Esther was a great beauty, a shrewd woman who became a great queen, probably accomplishing her greatest work as a teenager. Paul was the greatest of sinners who became the greatest of Apostles, used of God to write thirteen books of the New Testament.

So there are great people in the Bible. The Sovereign God both enables and allows people to achieve great things and thus be considered great in the eyes of history.

It's not so much the idea of greatness that should concern us, as it is our impulse toward greatness. An impulse is an inclination, or motive. It's the "why," and "for what," the desire of our heart that drives us.

While growing up,

As a child,

Danu used to hear his father tell him,

Every day,

"Danu, today you do greatness!"

Excellence As Greatness

God commands us to work for him, not just for employers or ourselves. He wants our work to be vigorous, reliable, and characterized by excellence. Anything less is dishonorable to the God who made us, the God who "worked" in creating the universe, who called his work "very good."

Excellence is, therefore, not an option, because excellence in what we do is one way we tell the world who God is. Excellence is a singular expression of biblical Christianity. Excellence in our relationships and excellence in our work are spiritual acts of worship before God. Excellence is the Christian way of doing things.

Doing all things excellently is no guarantee that you will achieve greatness in the annals of history. It is a guarantee that you will please God, serve him and others well, and bring blessings upon your life.

Oh, and by the way . . .

your greatness,

it might just be for something

much bigger . . . much much bigger,

and for something

larger

than yourself.

Greatness For The Glory Of God

So is it wrong to wish and work for greatness? It depends upon your motives (Jeremiah 45:5). The difference between unworthy and worthy greatness is the difference between selfish ambition and godly aspiration.

If you do greatness simply for personal aggrandizement, than you're headed for possibly "successful" experiences (in the view of contemporary culture), but ones that will inevitably lead to emptiness. This is true not because success per se is "bad" but because success based on selfish motives is transitory and unsatisfying. To test this, all you need to do is watch a few A&E, MTV, or Biography Channel "up close and personal" examinations of those who have achieved greatness qua selfishness. More often than not, the subjects end with broken dreams, broken promises, and broken lives.

If "Today you do greatness" for the glory of God, then you are headed for an experience that may or may not include fame and fortune but most certainly will include contentment and fulfillment. And that is greatness.

Godeep sent Danu to the United States for college

to get educated

in the American way,

to become a businessman.

To become a great leader.

And to return to India someday to teach greatness to his

people . . .

While at the University,

Danu woke each morning, dressed,

drank a glass of freshly-squeezed Florida orange juice,

glanced into the mirror,

and said, "Today Danu do greatness."

Greatness and Leadership

Greatness and leadership are not one in the same. It's possible to achieve greatness without being a leader in any conventional sense of the term. Consider nurse statistician Florence Nightingale, actor Jimmy Stewart, or world-renowned cellist Yo-Yo Ma. It's certainly possible to be a leader, even a recognized or "successful" one, without achieving greatness in the best sense of the term. Think Lyndon B. Johnson, Spiro Agnew, Pete Rose, or even Martha Stewart.

Interestingly, one of the things that made George Washington great was his eagerness to walk away from leadership. The late historian Stephen E. Ambrose said of Washington: "He voluntarily yielded power. His enemy, George III, remarked in 1796, as Washington's second term was coming to an end, 'If George Washington goes back to his farm he will be the greatest character of his age.' Napoleon, then in exile, was as stunned as the rest of the world by Washington's leaving office. He complained that his enemies 'Wanted me to be another Washington.' George Will noted, 'the final component of Washington's indispensability was the imperishable example he gave by proclaiming himself dispensable.'"

Great leaders know when to leave.

On weekends

Danu would sleep in late.

Rise and stretch.

Stare into the mirror,

deciding whether to shave.

And say to himself:

"No, not today. But Danu still do greatness."

"Great" But Evil

Greatness comes in different packages. It typically means highly accomplished, surpassingly effective in achieving goals, and attaining renown. This greatness may exist without benefit of moral judgment. In other words, with this definition—in the worse case examples— Hitler and Stalin achieved a kind of greatness even as they became purveyors of evil to an extent the world had never known. Was Alexander the Great really great?

History has a rogue's gallery of mostly men and some women who may have achieved "great" things, but who were not great people or great leaders. Nero, Attila the Hun, England's Queen "Bloody" Mary, Elizabeth Bathory the "Blood Countess" of Hungary, Idi Amin, Sadam Hussein, Muammar Gaddafi. So it makes us think. Is it really possible to do or to achieve greatness if we lack character, if we harm others, or if our ambition to do greatness knows no moral boundaries?

All in all,

Danu decided, greatness means many things.

But mostly, for Danu, greatness

Was synonymous with professional

Advancement.

And he noticed that for a lot of people,

It didn't much matter how you played the game,

Only that you won.

"Great" But Good

You see, greatness may also mean "good," or "right," thus denoting moral propriety and approval. In this definition, to be great one must also be good, or at least do good, for the benefit of others. With this added dimension we might think of John and Abigail Adams, "Honest Abe" Lincoln, or Andrew Carnegie. So our perception of greatness may be based upon an almost limitless variety of human achievements made possible by changing culture, while simultaneously based upon a very limited, nearly unchanging understanding of character.

Greatness in leadership is not simply about position, power, or personality. It's more about purpose, passion, and people. A person's fast-track drive, talent, or opportunity can take him or her to the top job and maximum dollars in the company. But if this career path is based upon nothing more than position, power, or personality, eventually the shine will come off the rose, causing it to wither, blight, or die—rich perhaps, but unloved and unsung.

If on the other hand, the same career path, to some extent, conveys a sense of shared purpose, generates passion for not only "doing things right but doing the right things," and cares about people, it will not simply survive. It will thrive. As an example, consider America's first female African-American millionaire Madam C. J. Walker, or think of Martin Luther King, Jr., Anwar Sadat and Manachem Begin, or Nelson Mandela.

Danu did greatness as he

was taught,

by studying, working, achieving,

climbing the corporate ladder.

he did greatness for stature,

for satisfaction, for wealth,

for himself.

And maybe for Godeep.

Greatness as a Calling

As we've noted, God calls people to a life of obedience, service, and excellence. Sometimes Bible scholars refer to this call to devotion as our "primary call."

Bible scholars also talk about a "secondary call." This doesn't typically happen via a burning a bush or writing on the wall or by some other miraculous life-changing experience.

Actually, God calls all of us first to be, then to do. What we do flows from what we've chosen to be—who we are—not the other way around. God calls us to a life of commitment to his will. That's our primary call. God also gives us natural (at physical birth) and spiritual (at spiritual re-birth) gifts, and he delights in our making sound moral choices about how to use these gifts to fulfill the calling in our lives, to do good works as to the Lord.

God allows us to fulfill our primary calling through a near infinite number of secondary callings. He knows that if Christ is truly preeminent in all that we do, than we can honor God with our talents by farming, teaching, homemaking, or preaching. We can honor God in politics, business, music and the arts, athletics, humanitarian or religious service, the military, and more.

Among all the possible jobs you can pursue, there is nothing you may choose to do that is any lesser or lower in the eyes of God than any other form of employment (assuming it is morally appropriate).

God's calling liberates us from human estimations of relative prestige. God's calling to devotion allows us to apply God's Word in life and culture. God's calling should protect us from the danger of arrogance and self-righteousness based upon our chosen professions.

Doing God's calling, living God's calling, empowers us to pursue a chosen profession with enthusiasm and energy and with godly ambition to accomplish great things as unto the Lord. If God allows us to experience any sense of greatness in our lifetimes, than it is but another gift to be used in his employ.

Someone once said, "America is great because America is good." The same is true for you and me. We cannot be truly great without goodness, but the Bible tells us there is none righteous except Jesus. So if we have godly aspirations to worthy forms of greatness (e.g., achievements "as working for the Lord," Colossians 3:23-24), we must first align our character with God's moral expectations.

Danu graduated with honors, an MBA, and worked,

entry level, at a small but promising company,

waking every morning, peering into the mirror,

and stating:

"Today Danu do greatness."

While in America, Danu did greatness

and practiced some rules for good living:

Build your career.

Trust no one but yourself.

Do whatever enhances your prospects.

Your greatness is about you.

Save, invest, manage your money well.

Maximize for your own benefit.

Take care of the investors

and they will take care of you.

Greatness is part power—part profit.

Profit matters most . . . go for the kill.

Work hard, Godeep would add, be loyal to yourself.

Above all, do greatness.

After all, the American cinema tells it all—Pretty Woman,

Wall Street, something about Howard Hughes . . .

Within three quick years

Danu was a director, then vice president,

and then executive vice president

of this once small,

but promising company.

Godeep was proud of his son's greatness.

Danu and three others were then considered for the chief

greatness opportunity,

President and Chief Executive Officer

of the organization.

Greatness Opportunity

Michelangelo said, "The greatest danger for most of us is not the fact that our aim is too high and we miss it, but that it is too low and we reach it." This quote is appealing for a lot of reasons, one of them being that Michelangelo's aim reached as high as the Sistine Chapel's ceiling.

Michelangelo was a talented superstar. His genius enabled him to attain heights most of us will never reach. But still, most of us have a lot going for us. Have you ever really met a truly one-talent person? God's abundant blessing is too limited for that. Most people are either multi-talented or maxi-talented. Most of us possess more talent than we realize—and dare we say, most of us do not use all the talent we've been given.

But Michelangelo's point is not really about talent. He's suggesting that most of us are too risk-averse, too limited in our vision, too willing to accept a small view of God, too insecure in our sense of what God has given us, or maybe just too lazy to reach high enough to test the talents we've been given. If this is true, then most people really don't attain the level of achievement and fulfillment God intended for them.

While applying for the Chief

Greatness Opportunity,

Danu considered briefly

many of his childhood friends

back in India.

He recalled how good they were,

but also how they lost

greatness . . .

vision . . .

and therefore

potential.

Lost Potential

Here is a sad commentary, one that rings true. It's a story of opportunity lost and a tale of what might have been. Consider your hometown or neighborhood. Think about old high school acquaintances who are still "just hanging out," having made little or no attempt to further their education or develop their skills; two or more failed marriages; seemingly satisfied to make do and muddle through; unwilling to take charge of their lives; eager for short-term destructive satisfactions—"Get drunk, get high, or get more."

Consider the pain, problems, and penury that often result from such poor choices.

Now consider your old high school acquaintances' untapped talent. Consider the undiscovered discoveries, the un-invented inventions, the unexpressed artistry, or the un-researched knowledge. Consider the lost potential represented in wasted time, talent, and treasure.

Do you really want to go through life with unused talents? Or would you much rather reach for the next level and see what God might do?

Danu also knew that his talents

were his own.

Honed through hard work,

determination,

discipline.

He owned his abilities,

possessed his talents.

And, unlike his childhood friends,

he used them wisely.

Using Talents

Alexander Graham Bell aimed high. In 1876 his first message over his new telephone was, "Mr. Watson. Come here. I want to see you." When Mr. Watson heard him, the 29-year-old Bell rushed to the appropriate government office with his phone patent, beating a competitor by only a few hours and launching an invention that would change communication into the Twenty-First Century. The next year he married Mabel and formed the Bell Telephone Company, thereby providing his family with a substantial income for the rest of their lives.

Blessed with an abiding intellectual curiosity, Alexander Graham Bell developed and tested ideas for kites, sheep breeding, desalinization techniques, water distillation, and a metal breathing device, forerunner of the iron lung.

Bell invented a "photophone," a device transmitting sound over a beam of light. He considered the photophone his most important invention, perhaps for good reason, for it became a precursor to modern laser and fiber optics technology. Bell spent the latter years of his life working on flight machines, and his hydrofoil set a water speed record in 1919 that remained unsurpassed until 1963.

Alexander Graham Bell's greatness was not his goal; rather, discovery and invention were his goals. But he became a great American scientist and success story because he used all of his considerable talents. He took risks and he worked diligently. He developed and applied his vision for a different tomorrow.

Through it all he remained a man of notable character and he helped untold thousands of people.

Because he worked so hard to grow and to develop his abilities,

Danu struggled with giving

anything back—to others,

or to his community.

After all

it is Danu who sacrificed.

His accomplishments and possessions were all about him.

Proactive Stewardship

"Proactive" is a word Alexander Graham Bell would have understood and it's a word every follower of God should learn. It means taking action based upon forward thinking. It means we should not just react to circumstances; we should pro-act. We should act with awareness. We should think innovatively and progressively. We should to try to anticipate changes in culture and seek to influence them. Better yet, we should to lead, not just respond.

Being proactive is what God talked about in the New Testament book of Matthew (24:42-51, 25:1-30). In a series of four parables God says that he expects us to be watchful, ready, wise, faithful, and working. In other words, in the time that he gives us on this earth God wants us to do something for him. He wants us to be active in his service, because he will hold us accountable for our work. He gives us life, creativity, and resources to use according to his rules for good living. It's a form of stewardship— proactive stewardship.

Being proactive stewards as a way of life prevents us from falling into ruts. We keep fixing our eyes on Jesus, and we keep pressing on to what he has in store for us. We keep following his rules for good living and expecting his will to be accomplished in our lives.

By becoming proactive stewards we can all do greatness for God, no matter what title appears in front of our name or what letters appear after.

Remember, Jesus's followers had no credentials or marketable skills . . . other than to follow and learn from his show and tell.

Danu won the position of chief greatness,

President and CEO,

and the others didn't.

He was the only one seeking power.

The day after his appointment, the value of his company

crumbled.

Stock went south due to oil prices, old wars, and the threat

of new wars.

Something about the Middle East.

Share owners took a bath.

Danu's company lost millions.

When Danu tried to explain this to his father,

Godeep responded:

    "As you know, in India we take bath every so

often as well. It is a part of living."

Belief Matters

Kurt Cobain was Nirvana's lead singer, a pioneering screamer of the Grunge rock scene. He was a fatalist, a nihilist. He believed life itself was absurdly without meaning. This was his model for good living. But in the end, which came to him all too soon, the sad illogic of his logic led him to kill himself with a shotgun.

Yet even today, several years following his death, his face still adorns t-shirts lining the walls of teen and young adult souvenir shops.

There's something very interesting about biblical Christianity that those who do not follow the Christian faith do not understand. God created men and women in his own image: reasoning, creative, eternal souls. He gave every human being who has ever lived at least three gifts: life, distinctive talents, and value. Consequently, whether people acknowledge God's gifts, every human being mirrors the Divine and "borrows" God's gifts every day.

This is as true in leadership or rules for good living as in any other area of life. People can employ a certain model of leadership that, along with their drive and talent, empowers them all the way to the top of their profession. They may pursue certain lifestyles that seemingly enable them to enjoy all that the world has to offer. Yet in whatever ways those models fail to align with biblical principles, they will be deficient, and someday those deficiencies inevitably become apparent.

Sadly, Kurt Cobain did not learn in time to save his own life that he mattered to God and that there was light and life, healing and hope to be found in him. What we believe matters.

Danu's vice presidents, three of them, served long,

productive careers,

loyal to Danu,

but without ever really coming to know much about Danu,

other than he followed rules for good living.

Only one other employee,

an office assistant named Esther,

Ever attempted to know Danu.

Danu was always curious about her,

but never

inquisitive.

He kept to himself,

though noticing the scrolling message on her computer

screen whenever she was away:

  "My saver is my Savior"

rolling, continuously, over and over,

whenever she was away

but yet still here.

Lifestyle Matters

By the time Iron Mike Tyson was 20 years old he was the Heavyweight Champion of the World—with all the fame and fortune that typically goes with it. But by the time he was 26 years old he was sentenced to six years in prison for raping a woman in a hotel room. After paying his debt to society he was once again allowed to fight professionally.

But by the time he was 31 years of age he was disqualified from boxing for biting off a piece of Evander Holyfield's ear during a fight. These are just the highlights.

Here was a world-class athlete, a man with a special gift, who by his choices was literally destroying his life and the lives of those unfortunate enough to get close to him. The deficiencies of his lifestyle model had been apparent since he was first arrested at 12 years of age. As Mike said, "I'm not Mother Teresa, but I'm not Charles Manson either." True, but saying you're not Manson is not much of a recommendation for your character. Mike needed help.

Today, Mike's a 40-something husband and father of eight. Having lost millions he makes a living as he can. He admits he's still troubled, but he's now stable enough to be grateful he has any life and family at all and spends time with his hobby, raising homing pigeons.

Without a change from the inside out Mike's future remains uncertain. Has he really matured? He knows he needs to be different than what he used to be, but he still needs help discovering how to make that happen. He's not Iron Mike anymore. Now, he's just Mike, and no one wants to be like Mike.

Danu wanted badly

to learn

rules for

good living.

Rules For Good Living

Lifestyle models that encompass our own set of rules for good living are powerful influencers. Think about Mickey Mantle. Young Mickey was born to play baseball. By the time he was 20 years old this strong farm kid from Oklahoma was playing for the New York Yankees. By the time he was 25 years old he had won baseball's Triple Crown, leading the league with a .353 batting average, 52 homeruns, and 130 RBIs. By the time he had finished his baseball career he had blasted 536 homeruns, third all-time in his day, had played in 12 World Series (Count them: 12!), and was one of the most popular players in the history of the game.

But for much of that career Mickey's rules for good living included unfettered excess: alcoholism, drug abuse, and womanizing—with its associated physical maladies. After a failed liver transplant he died of inoperable cancer at 63 years of age.

Just before Mickey Mantle died, though, he made two memorable choices. He made a video in which his emaciated body is clearly visible, looked into the camera, told viewers about his poor choices, and then said, "Don't be like me." It is one of the saddest videos you will ever see. It's a powerful summative comment on the results of a deficient lifestyle model.

Mickey Mantle made one more momentous choice. According to the testimony of his good friend and former playing partner Bobby Richardson, Mickey Mantle placed his faith in Jesus Christ for the forgiveness of his sins and therefore was promised entry into heaven. As he lay dying, Mickey asked God to change him from the inside out, to give him a new reason for living and an assurance of his destiny. Mickey Mantle got the help he needed. Though his life was near its end, Mickey embraced new rules for good living.

Danu's increasing success bought him increasing income.

He accumulated.

He became rich.

His bankers thought he was greatness.

Steward or Squander

Brains, beauty, strength, speed, or extraordinary physical coordination, professional success, fame, fortune, material abundance, power, position, and more—none of these otherwise useful attributes, resources, or accomplishments is necessarily evidence of good leadership or otherwise guarantees a good life.

While none of these attributes, resources, or achievements is morally suspect in themselves, none of them automatically results in greatness either. As gifts from God, all of them can be stewarded, or all of them can be squandered.

Tragically, Kurt Cobain squandered his life and talent. Tiger Woods risked his world-class athletic gifts on a series of adulterous flings, and it still remains to be seen how he proceeds with the rest of his life. Mike Tyson made egregious choices earlier in life and is now trying to live differently, but one wonders if he's attempting this in his own strength or with any understanding of the forgiving, enabling Spirit of God. Mickey Mantle, led by example at the end, figured out very late in his short life what really matters, but thankfully, not too late.

These were Danu's father's rules,

but Danu lived them out.

And there were more:

> Stay far from trouble, but close to profit.
>
> Stay close to your business, but far from debt.
>
> Stay on top of your people.
>
> Get good parking.

"Good parking," Godeep would remind him, "is

very, very important in America."

At 33 years of age

Danu was at the top of the corporate ladder,

waking every morning,

doing his routine,

seeing himself in the mirror before he left for the office,

and reciting:

"Today Danu do greatness."

And then he drove his sports car to his good parking.

Greed

*It's possible to work too much for the wrong reasons.
It's possible to be motivated by what Bill Hybels calls "the
monster called 'More,'" which is to say, greed.*

*This thing called greed is not a uniquely American
problem, but it's clearly one of our problems. Greed
happens when we go over the top with our work ethic. We
work at good projects for a good organization. We take
care of our family. We advance in our professions. We're
amazed at all the stuff we've acquired. But we still want
more.*

*Greed is not a word you expect to see listed among the
top ten rules for good living. You won't hear a preacher
in the midst of wedding vows encourage a couple to
pursue greediness. You won't hear any eulogies listing
greediness as one of the deceased's most endearing
qualities.*

*In one of the better-known passages of the Bible, God
talks about greed in what's often been called the "Parable
of the Rich Fool" (Luke 12:13-21). In this story the rich
fool celebrates his riches not with praise to God but with a
bold declaration to build even bigger barns for his goods.
Then he issues his infamous cry of excess: "Take life easy;
eat, drink, and be merry."*

*But earlier in the story, Jesus offered this divine
warning: "Watch out! Be on your guard against all kinds
of greed, a man's life does not consist in the abundance of
his possessions."*

Greed displaces the joy of work. Greed is a form of idolatry. Greedy people worship both conspicuous consumption and accumulation of assets more than God himself. Greedy people do not acquire-to-live; they live to acquire. What do they want? More. How much more? Just one more.

Greed equates life with what Jesus called "the abundance of his possessions." Greedy people define themselves based upon how much they have and how much more they can acquire---this could be money, personal property, net worth, corporate kingdoms, real estate, a greater inheritance . . . things. For men, it could even be wives (plural), "trophy wives," girlfriends, or just conquests. For women, it could be husbands (plural), boyfriends, or just lovers.

Howard Hughes was a brilliant man who wanted and seemingly attained it all. Greed warped his work and legacy. He died a spiritually bereft and psychologically disturbed man, lonely and alone.

For all this, greed isn't about "things" as much as it's about power or perceived stature. We want, not because we want the possession. We want because of what we think the possession can do for us or what the possession makes of us. This can be true whether the greedy person is a pauper or a tycoon. For a greedy person the amount is always relative.

Or, we want because of insecurity . . . in ourselves . . . in our lives . . . in our view of God.

Greed enslaves; it doesn't liberate. Under the guise of giving us more, greed instead exacts a price. Ironically, what we want to get actually takes from us.

The remedy for greed is to replace this form of idolatry in our hearts with a right expression of worship. Pursue God, not greed. Pursue work to the glory of God not the accumulation of possessions, power, or position. Pursue God not money-for-money's-sake. Pursue legitimate productivity and profit, i.e., money, in terms of God's calling. Pursue God and he will bless according to his sovereign will.

For all greed promises it only results in emptiness. For all God promises he fills our cup to overflowing.

Through the years many never succeeded in Danu's organization.

People he started out with left,

or were asked to leave.

Settlements were involved.

People who just couldn't cut it.

The culture.

Six people accepted early retirements,

a kind way of the corporation saying,

time to move on.

Most moved on to different careers altogether.

But not Danu.

His goal was to do greatness,

every day,

where he was.

Where he worked.

Location.

Job title.

Position.

It wouldn't have mattered.

Greatness was the thing to do. No matter what you did.

A clerk at 7-11.

A bagger at Wal-Mart.

Didn't matter.

Work Ethic

For nearly fifty years, Dr. Peter Roget refined the system of verbal classification that ultimately led in 1852 to the publication of An American Dictionary of the English Language.

William Wilberforce succeeded in making slavery illegal in the British Empire only after 50 years of political labor in the British Parliament.

Elizabeth Caty Stanton worked all of her adult life for women's suffrage, a cause finally embraced, after her death, largely because of her influence.

Thomas Edison conducted experiments with thousands of filaments, trying to find one that would glow brightly with longevity, before successfully inventing a practical incandescent light bulb.

Nadia Comeneci said, "To have that gold medal around your neck, it takes ten years of work."

Rome wasn't built in a day. Work that's worthwhile requires time and effort.

When God placed Adam and Eve in the Garden of Eden he gave them the tasks of naming the animals and caring for the garden. God established work before sin came along to spoil the scene. Work is not a result of the curse of sin. Work is associated with creation, with the very image of the Creator God within each human being.

To learn to work is to learn to create. To learn to work is to learn to invest one's vision and talents in natural materials and thus to produce a thing of value. To learn to work well is always to experience satisfaction and fulfillment and typically to enjoy a certain amount of material blessing.

The Old Testament Proverbs contain numerous references to work ethic, for example, "Lazy hands make a man poor, but diligent hands bring wealth" (Proverbs 10:4). Of course not all poverty is the result of individual laziness, but neither is laziness something to be condoned or reinforced, either by Church or State. In the New Testament, God says, "If a man will not work, he shall not eat" (2 Thessalonians 3:10).

A good work ethic meets basic needs and is a path to accomplishment. You don't have to be a rocket scientist. To achieve, you only need God-given talent—which all of us possess—coupled with a willingness to work. Your talent is intrinsic. Your work ethic is a choice.

The way God designed the world a person who is lazy and does not work will reap less, not more. In God's economy, work is both good and good for you. Work is not always fun or easy, but it's still good. A strong work ethic is therefore not only admirable but also a blessing to you, your family, your organization, and your community.

Your good work ethic benefits everyone.

Working hard is

Just

What you do,

Danu says.

Why even think about it (hard work)?

Work

At the zenith of his tennis success John McEnroe hated to practice. He practiced, sure, but not nearly as much as other top tier players. To prepare for tournaments he'd hit the ball in doubles matches. But he didn't want to grind it out in practice—and he still won his share of majors. He was a world-class talent and one of the very rare examples of someone who seemingly could get away with cutting corners.

For at least the first part of his career Tiger Woods was also All-World in his sport, a naturally gifted athletic talent evident from early childhood. But Woods built upon his talent. He practiced as often, as diligently, and as intensely as anyone in the history of professional golf. He continually tried to perfect his already powerful swing. He developed his body, adding strength and stamina. He ate correctly and he studied courses and the game. During his first years on the tour he single-handedly changed the practice work ethic among PGA tour players. Top golfers adopted Woods's practice regimen, developing stronger bodies and sharper skills.

Maybe if Johnny Mac had practiced more than he argued with umpires he would've won more majors. Maybe if John Daly had adopted a disciplined approach to the game, and his life, he'd have toned his body, avoided self-indulgent excess in alcohol, gambling, and more, and possibly won more tournaments early in his career.

"Hard work never hurt anyone," our grandfathers said, and they were right. Work ought to be an enjoyable blessing in our lives.

Valuing work was first a biblical ideal and only later a concept borrowed by businesses and political party platforms. Both work and rest were ordained by God "in the beginning" when he created the universe in six days and rested on the seventh.

Work is part of God's design for happy and productive lives. When it's rightly understood and performed for the right reasons, work brings satisfaction. Work is a positive, integral, and fulfilling part of human existence. It's part of the divine plan.

When you hear someone whining or complaining about his or her work it's a danger signal. Something is out of alignment.

God's working model of productive excellence followed by restorative rest is both a limitation and a blessing we must follow today. It's a limitation in that we cannot physically or mentally maintain an around-the-clock pace. For short intervals, yes, and sometimes for extraordinary accomplishments we push beyond our limits. But eventually we must rest. This is one way God reminds us of our finitude. It's one way the Spirit of God restrains the evil humanity could bring upon itself if no rest was needed.

But it's also a blessing. God built into human beings a need and desire for rest for our own good. Rest periods give us time to focus upon other priorities, including our families. Rest periods provide us with a physical and mental distance from our work, allowing us to reflect, to sharpen objectivity, to see things we would not otherwise see.

Rest does not necessarily mean a suspension of all physical or mental activities. It means pursuing different activities, like hobbies, recreation, or relationships. Recreation is also a way for re-creation. Rest means time with God, spent alone with him, an opportunity to gather together with others of like faith to enjoy the restorative powers of this thing called "fellowship." Rest is a gift from God who wishes for us the best of all his creation.

Today, a Sunday, Danu was feeling lonely in America

so he bought a dog.

He named his dog, simply, "No,"

since that is what he found himself saying so much.

"No" this . . . "No" that . . . "No!"

Over the years, Danu supported his family in India,

sending modest sums of money each month,

and visiting on occasion.

When at home,

in New Delhi,

a city of millions of people,

Danu's father and grandfather

would wake each morning,

give Danu a big hug,

and say to him: "Sacred cow important.

Parking more important.

But Danu today

You do greatness."

While in America,

and not in the office,

Danu kept to himself.

He lost interest in India,

something his father, Godeep, blamed on

Americanism.

Sundays Danu slept in,

relaxed,

unshaven,

read the Wall Street Journal.

He studied the stocks.

And he told No, "No!"

for taking the Sports before he had the chance to read it.

But mostly Danu took long walks

and thought of ways to,

come Monday,

return clean shaven to the office

in order to practice doing more

greatness.

Rest

Living for our jobs is a danger all of us face, especially leaders who bear greater responsibilities. And especially leaders who want to do greatness.

Learning to balance work and rest is a process for most of us. We don't come by it naturally. We've been taught to work. We want success. We aspire to greatness, and we often think work is the only means of achieving it. But a former long-time university president, Dr. W. Wilbert Welch, once said, "You only have one body. Whatever you do for the Lord, you do it in that body. So if you burn out the body you'll never accomplish as much for the Lord. You must rest." Words like this from a healthy octogenarian and accomplished leader carry a lot of weight.

Rest and laziness are not synonymous. Rest rejuvenates. Rest reinforces our work, while laziness undermines it. Rest combined with exercise is a powerful restorative to the body and the mind.

Ronald Reagan would go to his ranch in Santa Barbara and chop wood. This was more than a photo-op for the seventy-something president. It was his way of getting exercise and working out his frustrations. At the height of the tension in the buildup to D-Day, General Dwight Eisenhower would take naps. Until his knees weakened, former President George W. Bush was a runner. Now he's a trim bicyclist.

Rest, and the recreation that is sometimes part of it, matter because our health and our work matter.

Productive excellence—restorative rest—and repeat. That's God's recipe for life in the real world.

On his way to work one day

Dan heard a radio offer to tour Israel,

find God,

for only $3,250.

All meals included.

He thought it was a bargain until he learned about the 50%

non-refundable deposit that was required.

Always a catch, he thought, in finding God.

Until Danu heard the commercial,

he didn't know that God lived in Israel,

he thought to himself,

smiling with a bit of sarcasm.

Looking For Zacchaeus

Not long after the Berlin Wall fell in 1989, a group of sixteen Christian educators from America traveled to the Soviet Union to discuss the possibility of founding a new Christian university in that country. For the first three days members of the group were amazed at how many Russians professed to be "believers." The Christian educators thought, "It seems like everyone we meet is a believer. Are there really this many Christians in Russia?"

It took awhile for the Americans to discern that what their new Russian friends were really saying was "I am not one of those godless Communists you've heard about." They meant what we would mean if we said: "I'm religious." The Russian hosts knew their guests were Christian educators, and they were trying to communicate that they believed in God and shared an interest in religious faith, points of view that had been suppressed by the Soviet regime.

Once this became clear to the American educators they began to gently tell their Russian friends about the special meaning Christians assign to the word "believer"—that it is more than an acknowledgement of God and faith—it is a personal acceptance of Jesus Christ as Lord and Savior. The Americans didn't have to learn to speak Russian. They did have to learn to speak cross-culturally: not American to Russian as much as Christian to non-Christian. They needed to learn "Zacchaeus's culture."

Zacchaeus, you may recall, was a chief tax collector, a wealthy man of small stature who lived in Israel at the time of Christ (Luke 19:1-10). His height never mattered much until one red-letter day in his life. That's the day when Zacchaeus's height prevented him from seeing Jesus as the Savior walked through Jericho in the midst of a large crowd. Smart man that he was, Zacchaeus ran ahead and climbed a sycamore-fig tree with branches overhanging the path Jesus walked. When Jesus reached a spot under the tree, he looked up and said, "Zacchaeus, come down immediately. I must stay at your house today."

This declaration shocked the crowd, to say the least, and the people began muttering rather self-righteously, "He has gone to be the guest of a sinner."

But Jesus said, "Today salvation has come to this house . . . for the Son of Man came to seek and to save what was lost."

Jesus wasn't repelled by Zacchaeus's status as a sinner. Rather he was compelled by it. Jesus knew Zacchaeus was a sinner in need of grace (like all of us and like the Jericho crowd too), so he went looking for him. Jesus didn't find Zacchaeus in the synagogue. He found Zacchaeus outside, up a tree. Had Jesus only spent time with the religious, and had Jesus only given himself to the righteous, he would never have met Zacchaeus. Jesus looked for a sinner needing grace where he knew he'd find him—among the general public, in the marketplace, in the real world.

Like Jesus, to be able to share their faith winsomely, those Christian educators had to "look for Zacchaeus" and learn to speak Christian ideals into the non-Christian culture of their hosts.

Danu's company

began to flourish.

To thrive.

Employees were happy.

Shareholders were happier.

The board of directors was elated.

When he first began working at his company,

now 36 years ago,

many of Danu's colleagues invited him to their bars on

Saturdays,

and to their churches on Sundays.

Danu wondered why there were so many churches in

America.

And bars.

And he found it amusing why people didn't just

stay far from trouble.

Stay close to your business.

Stay on top of your people.

Stay focused.

And Danu wondered

why Americans must pay

$3,250 to go

directly to where God lived.

Danu declined, politely, each kind invitation,

to both the bars

and the churches.

And after a while they stopped asking.

On Mondays he continued to apply leadership practices

And rules for good living

in order to do greatness.

God Talk

Many of our neighbors and workplace associates are like Zacchaeus: hard working, successful in a variety of ways but spiritually up a tree of their own making. Except for a few weddings and funerals, many of our neighbors and associates haven't been in a church in years. They don't know church language, "God talk," or Christian jargon. In fact, it makes them uncomfortable. They don't know what fellowship means, and they wouldn't recognize a baptistry, a nave, or a narthex if they saw one. They wouldn't know when to stand up and when to sit down during a church service, nor would they know the difference in a consistory, a parish, or a congregation.

They don't know how churches are different or why there are so many of them. They sometimes misjudge biblical Christianity because they equate the bad behavior of some Christians with the Christian faith. They think churches just want their money. In fact, ironically enough, they wouldn't go to church if you paid them. They are Zacchaeus, spiritually up a tree but unwilling or unable to seek help in the church.

We therefore need to get outside the safety zones of our churches. We need to learn how our Christian faith speaks to the moral ambiguity of our culture and the social issues of our age.

What hope does biblical Christianity provide for the ill, the elderly, or the abandoned child? What healing message does God's Word offer to those struggling with sexual sin and brokenness, drugs, pornography, or gambling addiction? What does biblical Christianity say to sufferers and survivors of earthquakes and tsunamis, tornadoes, hurricanes, and floods? Is God still in charge of a world beset by war and terrorism? What do we say to friends caught in the Rat Race, running only for success, perhaps materially well off but spiritually unwell?

We need to know the answers to these and similar questions because they are the questions of Zacchaeus. We need to lead spiritually like so many books tell us to lead professionally—by example. We need to know truth and to make it known.

In the late nineteenth century, in the very early days of D. L. Moody's ministry, one of his close friends, Henry Varley, said: "It remains to be seen what God will do with a man who gives himself up wholly to him." Moody responded, "Well, I will be that man," and took this as his charge. Later in D. L. Moody's life he spoke from experience: "No one can sum up all God is able to accomplish through one solitary life, wholly yielded, adjusted, and obedient to him."

The greatest individuals in Scripture were men or women who simply obeyed God. The same was true in D.L. Moody's day, and the same is true in ours. Obedient men and women eagerly look for Zacchaeus.

Late that afternoon

Danu ran an errand for his housekeeper,

Josepha,

bailing her son out of jail.

No one else in the company ever knew.

Well-read, Danu knew basically, about

the 5 popular faiths.

Hinduism, of course. He is from India.

Buddhism.

Judaism.

Islam.

And Christianity.

Though he had no strong religious beliefs,

he was often confused at the commercialism of the

Christian

business

in America.

In time he had noticed the books,

the music,

the bracelets and t-shirts,

the preachers with big hair on TV,

the websites,

the bumper stickers,

the billboards,

and even the president of the United States,

all proclaiming Jesus.

"This business of Christianity," Danu once wrote his father

Godeep, "equals big industry. Very, very, much money.

And most likely

good parking."

A pop-up

on Danu's computer

one day informed him of a site

offering discounted religious advice

for the spiritually confused.

For only $19.95

per month,

an introductory rate,

you could find

inner peace.

A pop-up

on his father Godeep's computer

has never happened.

What is a computer, he asks.

Danu smiled at this,

deleted it,

and resumed doing

greatness.

Transformation

George Foreman was once a "Zacchaeus." He grew up poor and mean in Houston. As a junior high school drop out he heard a commercial in which football giant Jim Brown endorsed the Job Corps. Jim said to join the Job Corp if you wanted a second chance, so George joined. He began vocational training and boxing. He didn't like the boxing part. But his boxing coach liked him and told him that if he stopped fighting in the streets and alleys he could become an Olympic champion. George took up the challenge. He was still mean and tough, incredibly strong, and talented. By 1968, George realized his coach's dream by winning the heavyweight Gold Medal in Mexico City at just 19 years of age.

Today George is so well recognized that most people know the rest of the story—heavyweight boxing champion of the world—twice, the second time at 45 years of age, the oldest ever, one of the strongest men to ever throw a professional punch. Later, he became corporate spokesman for the George Foreman Grill and a host of other products. Further, he is one of the most effective and sought after corporate spokesmen in America. George is a very wealthy man—a rarity among ex-boxers, particularly since the bulk of his fortune comes from sources other than boxing—and he enjoys a stable family and ten children, famously all named some version of George.

How could a once scowling man known for meanness and violence become so likeable? It dates to 1977 when George was 28 years of age and had just lost a fight in

Puerto Rico. He went to his dressing room feeling utterly depressed and began thinking, for some reason, about dying. Not only was he scared to die, he thought we was going to die, and soon, in boxing. He'd always believed in some kind of God but not in religion. This large-body version of Zacchaeus was no churchgoer. For George, religion was for losers. But then again, top contender though he was, he too was a loser in a boxing match that very day. More importantly, he was a loser on the path of his life.

George has shared the testimony of his salvation the world over. He came to Christ that night, because Christ came to him in that dressing room. He gave his life to God, went home to Houston, became an ordained minister, and now regularly preaches in a small Baptist church in his home city. So radical was George Foreman's spiritual transformation—which immediately affected his attitude, demeanor, and lifestyle—that writers regularly refer to George I, the mean boxing George, and George II, the jovial guy that men respect and women like, the perfect combination for a preacher of the Gospel and a promoter of products.

Zacchaeus in this story was neither small nor Jewish. He was a very big, strong, tough African American at the peak of his physical prowess and at the bottom of his spiritual wellbeing. The moral of the story is that the Zacchaeuses in our sphere of influence can be anybody. We need to look for him or her, and we need to understand our own culture so we can communicate God's Word and will within it.

At a retirement dinner

that Danu's company hosted for his long-term manager,

Esther,

he hangs onto her parting remarks,

made before over 200 staff members:

"I have enjoyed my 29 years here.

I have also enjoyed Danu's greatness.

His wisdom in growing our company,

and his compassion and kindness.

Every day I have worked here."

At this Danu blushed slightly,

He acknowledged with his humble smile

how much he would miss Esther.

"But most of all I have enjoyed the fact

that Danu has accepted me for who I am."

Danu was surprised at this comment,

having no idea what Esther meant.

As he sat there Danu struggled with what to do.

What was next?

Great Leadership

Columnists, consultants, and scholars do not often agree. But an amazing consensus is emerging among the chattering classes regarding leadership. What America needs, according to these thinkers, are doers, which is to say, leaders with moral imagination. What America needs, in politics, business, education, religion, medicine, and every other corner of life are leaders who speak with moral clarity and courage.

America needs these kinds of leaders because the times in which we live are characterized by uncertainty, chaos and confusion. It's a time of rapid change, global competition, pandemics, intractable social problems, and technological imperatives advancing "high tech" at the expense of "high touch." In volatile times like these, individuals and nations become hungrier for leaders who provide answers—or at least hope.

President Theodore Roosevelt was such a man for such a time. He came to national prominence first as a New York assemblyman and as police commissioner of New York City, and then as governor of New York, assistant secretary of the Navy, colonel of the Rough Riders, and vice president, all before age 42. He first came to national, then international power when he was elevated to President of the United States upon the assassination of President William McKinley in 1901.

Roosevelt took office just after the turn of the century, at the height of the Industrial Age. Americans were experiencing the impact of a changing economy, an immense immigration movement, new inventions like the automobile and the airplane, a recent war with Spain and a brewing war in Europe. Roosevelt strode boldly upon the scene, fighting monopolies, creating national parks and advancing conservation, ending American isolationism and reinforcing military preparedness ("Speak softly and carry a Big Stick"), negotiating the peace of the Russo-Japanese War, and perhaps his crowning achievement, facilitating the building of the Panama Canal. He preached a "square deal" for all Americans. And he held the record for writing the most books of any president until he was later surpassed by Jimmy Carter.

Theodore Roosevelt was the quintessential doer, a leader with moral imagination, courage, and clarity of thought and speech. He may not have always been right, but he always gave his all and had a "bully time" of it. He did not fear the challenges of his times. He addressed them—and in most cases altered them.

President Theodore Roosevelt knew what he believed and why he believed it, which empowered him to lead with vision and vigor. He is, therefore, considered one of the greatest of American presidents, earning a unique place among the pantheon of America's greats on Mt. Rushmore.

One by one,

his people

began to stand.

Stating, one after another,

something like:

"Thank you, Esther, for being my leader."

"Thank you, Danu, for enabling Esther to be our leader."

"Thank you, Esther, for sharing your faith with me."

"Thank you, Esther, for teaching us about God. And how

he would have me be at work."

And "Thank you for teaching me that you can love.

Even at work.

Love others, I mean. As Christ Jesus loved
others."

And, frankly, "Thanks Esther, for helping me figure out

the God-part of my life."

One by one,

tall and applauding.

Until Danu looked around the banquet facility,

and all but he and three other people, were standing.

These were the same three who wanted to be CEO,
many, many years ago.

The thought then occurred to Danu

that Esther

had worked directly for him for nearly three decades.

That's over 1,300 weeks.

That's over 9,125 days.

And yet Danu hadn't known her.

He had no idea.

No idea of her faith.

No idea about the God-part.

No idea it was so strong.

No idea that she had shared the gospel and her Christian
worldview with over 200 co-workers.

No idea that she'd done anything other than keep the
company's books clean.

Never a bad audit.

Never a questionable business practice.

Never a complaint about her, Esther, or the company.

Esther was moved at the standing ovation,

seemingly for her,

and started to return to her seat

at the table's head,

next to Danu.

But then she stopped when a co-worker,

Benjamin,

stepped up to the podium and reached for the microphone.

In a small, meek voice,

Benjamin said:

> "In case you didn't know, the original Esther was
> an exiled Jew living in the Persian Empire. When
> Queen Vashti displeased King Xerxes, Esther was
> the one, chosen from among many beautiful young
> women, who won the heart of the king and became
> the new queen. Later, when a plot emerged to kill
> all the Jews, every single one, Esther was used by
> God to save her people."

Benjamin paused, then looked to Danu.

"I realize, Sir, that I am putting my job on the line

tonight, what with these personal remarks,

but when I started here six years ago

I was lost.

I was living in terrible circumstances.

And then I met Esther."

Benjamin's eyes turned moist with tears.

> "In the break room one day Esther introduced me
>
> to faith. Real faith—All I have to say tonight, Mr.
>
> Danu, is thank you for hiring Esther 19 years
>
> before I was hired here. Who knows but that you,
>
> Mr. Danu–just like Esther here–come to position
>
> 'for such a time as this'" (Esther 4:14).

And Benjamin took his seat.

And the evening ended with embraces and with words of

congratulations and tears. And testimonies about how,

specifically, Esther had worked in their lives.

And Danu and the three employees who didn't stand

returned home and called it a night.

Barnabas Salute

Some people are born encouragers, but most of us have to learn how to be encouraging to others. In the Bible, the word "encouragement" is drawn from a military term meaning "to strengthen, harden, or uplift." Encouragement means to meet people where they are and help them along to where they want to be or ought to be.

Usually we think of encouraging people who are "down," individuals who are experiencing some difficulty like financial pressures, interpersonal relationship problems, a mid-life crisis, loss of a loved one, or maybe just stress. But people also need encouragement when things are going very well, when they are "up." Think about it: if not many call or write when things are going poorly, think how few call or write when everything appears to be on a roll!

The biblical Joseph was a Levite from Cyprus who the Apostles nicknamed "Barnabas," which means "Son of Encouragement." Barnabas encouraged the Christians at Antioch and he's described as "a good man, full of the Holy Spirit and faith" (Acts 11:24). Barnabas lived up to his name.

Authentic, heart-felt encouraging is a high-impact leadership skill every leader should develop. Each leader should strive to be a Barnabas who looks for people to whom he or she can give a "Barnabas Salute," a call, a note, a pat on the back, any appropriate form of "Way to go." You can salute people you know or even people you don't know.

Giving people a Barnabas Salute is an encouragement to them, but guess what, it's an encouragement to you too.

The next morning Danu followed his routine.

He dressed, he drank a glass of freshly-squeezed Florida orange juice,

he glanced into his mirror.

But what came out of his mouth this day

was not, "Today Danu do greatness."

Instead Danu was speechless.

He was 55 years old and he felt empty.

He felt alone, even with his dog No obeying his every command.

Godeep had taught him much.

Danu had learned much.

And though he thought he knew something about faith,

he realized last night that he didn't know

the first thing

about faith.

Danu felt thirsty,

even though he'd just sipped his orange juice.

He was due to retire next year.

He was planning to return home,

to India,

to be with his family.

But he was determined to understand faith,

the God-part

missing from his faith.

He had been in America since he was 19 years old.

He had managed to lead a small company to greatness.

He hired hundreds of staff.

He had live in a neighborhood dense with families

for over 30 years.

And yet, he realized last night at Esther's retirement

that he didn't know a single neighbor.

He didn't really know a single employee.

Except for the three other people who,

like him,

couldn't stand,

for they were the only ones in the crowd whom Esther

hadn't touched.

They were the only ones in the crowd who wouldn't let

Esther touch them.

He knew three people.

He knew them, all right.

And though he knew them at about the same level as most

people

know their mailman,

he knew their hearts were like his–

lonely,

cold,

alone.

Danu learned in his MBA program that,

often,

as a leader your heart would be lonely.

Cold.

Alone.

And that the wealth you obtain due to your leadership,

and increasing responsibilities, could make you

lonelier.

Lonely Leadership

Leadership can be lonely, but ironically, you can't do it alone. Even the Lone Ranger had his trusted friend Tonto and his beloved horse Silver. Leaders who try to do it alone are either arrogant or foolish. Either way, they're typically doomed to falter or fail, professionally as well as personally.

There are different kinds of lonely. Leaders can work well with others, inspiring them to production and achievement, yet feel lonely in their own lives.

Lonely in a crowd. Lonely in a relationship. Maybe just alone. Or maybe achingly lonely at heart.

Danu,

lonely,

a warrior without an

obvious war,

lonely in his world,

Drives on . . .

Significance

Lonely—at least in the sense of being by oneself—is probably not a condition that the Old Testament King Solomon ever experienced. He was the center of attention for all of his adult life. He was, the Bible says, the wisest man who ever lived. He was king during Israel's Golden Age. He lived in regal splendor, enjoying an integrated experience of money, sex, and power that no current billionaire, sheik, political leader, or entertainment star could fathom. His life didn't need an "extreme makeover," because his life was already extreme. Solomon had everything!

Why then did he begin one of his books with the melancholy cry, "Meaningless! Meaningless! Utterly meaningless! Everything is meaningless" (Ecclesiastes 1:2)? Was this man hard to please? Or was he just like you, me, and the next person?

Even with everything, a success by any definition, Solomon knew something was missing. Solomon hungered for meaning, for significance. He needed to know that his life was worth something, that it wasn't just futility. Solomon wanted to know for sure that his life had lasting value. He wanted to know that there was more to life than work, possessions, and the grave. He wanted to know that somehow it all meant something. So do we.

Solomon used his position and privilege to search for meaning by testing and experiencing everything the world had to offer. With full and maybe wild abandon he tried knowledge, pleasure, wealth, material goods, work, politics, and the various religions of his day.

If this wasn't enough, Solomon is also remembered for his mind-boggling one thousand-woman harem. Solomon maintained three hundred wives and seven hundred concubines (an old word for a kind of mistress). This was more a testimony to his financial stature than his sexual prowess, but clearly Solomon explored the limit of emotional possibilities represented by companionship, romance, love, and sex.

After all these adventures—emotional, intellectual, and physical—Solomon summarized his findings this way: "I undertook great projects: I built houses for myself and I planted vineyards. I made gardens and parks and planted all kinds of fruit trees in them . . . amassed silver and gold for myself . . . denied myself nothing my eyes desired; I refused my heart no pleasure. My heart took delight in all my work, and this was the reward for all my labor. Yet when I surveyed all that my hands had done and what I had toiled to achieve, everything was meaningless, a chasing after the wind; nothing was gained under the sun" (Ecclesiastes 2:4-11).

Solomon discovered that where we frequently get off track is in worshipping various parts of the created order rather than the God who made them. Like Solomon, we too often try to do greatness by doing acquisition.

Danu

Was driven

Partly by

Having everything.

It is natural.

Yet, he surveys his

Work

And concludes,

I have it all . . .

Yet I can have more . . .

Acquisition and Accumulation

In the Old Testament book of Haggai, God warned his people about the false joys of miss-directed acquisition. He said, "Give careful thought to your ways. You have planted much, but have harvested little. You eat, but never have enough. You drink, but never have your fill. You put on clothes, but are not warm. You earn wages, only to put them in a purse with holes in it" (1:5-6).

The people of Haggai's time suffered from a blight of wrong priorities. They pursued things, their own ambitions, at the exclusion of the Lord's will for them, and therefore at all costs. In the end, they acquired neither things of lasting value nor happiness, yet it cost them the very time of their lives.

For all his abundance Solomon hungered for meaning. In abundance he thought he saw greatness, but without meaning nothing matters. Solomon learned that meaning comes only in a right relationship with the Sovereign Creator God. He learned that nothing else fills the hole in our hearts. Nothing else validates the eternal significance we sense in our souls but cannot attain by ourselves.

Meaning—and the peace and fulfillment that it generates—comes only when we comprehend and embrace who God is, who we are as his created beings, and what he has provided to reconcile us in relationship to him. Seeking meaning in anything else is what Solomon called "chasing after the wind."

It can never be caught.

Parenthetically, when the light went on for Solomon following all his philosophic experimentation, he did not burn or otherwise destroy all his worldly goods in some kind of ascetic trade for significance. He did not recommend downsizing by "living with less" or divestiture of all God had given him. He didn't go for broke, literally, and embrace poverty.

What Solomon did was put his motives, wealth, and material wellbeing in right relationship with God. He came to understand the world God has given us for development and culture as God had intended.

If not for the Lord, Solomon would be a tragic figure remembered for his hedonistic excess rather than his wisdom. But after a lifetime quest for meaning, Solomon wisely concluded, "Fear God and keep his commandments, for this is the whole duty of man" (Ecclesiastes 12:13-14).

In his native India there is a saying,

loosely translated:

"If an invisible man marries an invisible woman,

their son will be nothing to look at."

Today, Danu felt invisible.

He was very, very wealthy. But very, very lonely.

And alone.

Eventually, the words that finally came from Danu's

mouth while he was still staring at himself in the mirror

were these:

"Today Danu does greatness by not being invisible."

That day Danu did something he did not learn in his MBA

program.

He did not learn it in any textbooks,

or from any dynamic Fortune 500 speaker.

Rather, he called Esther and asked her to return to work.

But for only the day.

She did.

Steps To Greatness

Reverend Billy Graham is a truly singular individual. People who have met him, including former President George W. Bush, remember the occasion with respect akin to awe, not because of Billy's fame but because of his humble, godly spirit.

In over sixty years of worldwide ministry, no hint of scandal ever touched Billy Graham or the team of leaders surrounding him. No one absconded with organizational money, no one conducted clandestine affairs, no marriage ended in divorce, no one struggled with Billy for control of the organization, and no one left to create a competing organization. In other words, no one yielded to the lust of the eyes, the lust of the flesh, or the pride of life—or as we say it today, no one succumbed to the allure of money, sex, and power.

We're not suggesting Billy Graham and his supporting team never made mistakes. We're saying they submitted themselves to God's will and therefore the Lord blessed and protected them.

Very early in Billy's ministry, he and his team were conducting services in Modesto, California. One day Billy was greatly saddened to hear that a fellow evangelist had fallen into some grievous sin, causing the evangelist to leave the ministry. That evening, Billy instructed his team to go to their rooms, pray, write down everything they could identify that caused people to leave the ministry, and then gather later for a discussion. The result was what became known as "The Modesto Manifesto."

Today we'd call it a "Code of Ethics," but to Billy's team sixty years ago it was simply a list of common sense practices they embraced in their desire to reinforce personal holiness and to serve God faithfully. They agreed that Billy and the team would all receive an established salary from the organization and never "dip in" to crusade offerings. In fact, Billy regularly told reporters thereafter that he had no idea how much money had been received during area meetings. It was all handled by others.

They agreed to book rooms close together in hotels as a form of mutual accountability to protect their relationships with their spouses. They agreed never to allow Billy in particular to drive or be driven in a car alone with any woman other than his wife. They wanted to avoid even the "appearance of evil," as well as the opportunity for temptation. They sent staff members into Billy's hotel rooms first to assure that no one was secreted in the room in a manner that might cause embarrassment to Billy or the ministry. They agreed, as the ministry's ability to support them grew, that they would travel with their spouses as much as possible and that they would not be away from their spouses any longer than was absolutely necessary.

In Christian terms it should not be remarkable that a group of Christian people served God for several decades without hint of scandal. But in today's terms, it is.

Billy Graham is a leader recognized for his spiritual focus and his global impact. He is famous, and he has met the rich and famous. He is a powerful religious figure, and he has met the powerful. He is a leader who for decades successfully led an organization with a global reach. He is a compassionate man who knows his achievements are not really about him and are not his alone. He is not a perfect man, but he is a man who loves the Lord, loves the Word of God, and loves people. He is the rarest of creatures, a humble leader who truly has done and continues to do greatness.

The next year, as planned, Danu did indeed retire from his
company.

He returned to his homeland, India, with his dog No,
and with something he had never had before.

Danu returned home, to his family, with love dwelling in
his heart.

He had always followed the rules for good living,
but Danu returned to his home with something more.

Greatness In God's Will

In another time long ago, Moses was a leader a lot like Billy Graham. Moses is described in Scripture as the most humble man upon the face of the earth (Numbers 12:3). This is a fascinating fact. How is it possible that this humble man is also remembered as a great leader? How did he accomplish so many great things for God with such a humble spirit?

Despite Charlton Heston's larger-than-life portrayal of Moses in "The Ten Commandments" film, Moses was not a good speaker, lacked what today we'd call self-esteem, was at times a man of weak faith, and at 80 years of age was no spring chicken. When God called him to his task Moses repeatedly offered God excuses and asked him to send someone else. His most recent leadership experience was leading sheep. He was well educated, but the Egyptians considered him an outcast. Moses did not stride into Pharaoh's palace and demand the release of his people the Israelites because he possessed any personal power to enforce his will.

Actually, God said, "Go." Moses went. Moses said, "Go." And the people of Israel went. So began the Exodus and meek Moses's march into history as one of the greatest leaders the world has ever known.

Moses became a great leader because he submitted his will to God's will. Though the Scripture records Moses's mistakes, his pattern was obedience, humility, and faithfulness to his assigned task.

As Danu's family greeted him

and No

at the New Delhi International Airport,

Danu's father Godeep (now 88 years old) embraced him

with all the love that a father has for his son.

And then some.

Danu's family wept with joy at the return of their only son.

Eventually he looked his son in the eye and said:

"My Danu still do greatness!"

To which Danu replied:

"Yes, Father, but Danu do real greatness

for the very first time, in the name of love."

It was a long and awkward trip home from the

international airport,

for Danu and his family,

who repeatedly asked him:

"Danu, our son, you are different now?

You are not like us? No more?"

To which Danu repeatedly replied:

"No . . . No . . . Please understand . . ."

And the entire family was confused,

unsure if Danu was answering their question,

or just addressing his dog.

Danu spent the next few weeks trying to explain

to his family that he only recently discovered true

greatness,

in fact in his final year in business,

in America,

just before his leaving.

And that he learned the key to doing true greatness from

Esther.

The key to doing true greatness was love.

Meek Greatness

We know that humility, meekness, or gentleness as it is variously translated in different versions of Scripture is something all Christian people are commanded to develop (1 Timothy 6:11). Scripture even tells us "Blessed are the meek, for they will inherit the earth" (Matthew 5:5). But meekness and leadership don't seem to fit together—that is, until you understand more about both meekness and leadership.

Meekness does not mean weakness. It does not mean ineffectiveness, indecisiveness, fearfulness, or lack of confidence. Meekness means a quiet sense of one's own limits and a developed sense of one's dependency upon God and others.

Leadership, on the other hand, is not about self-aggrandizement and personal power—at least good leadership is not about these things. The best form of leadership maximizes the contributions of others. It seeks to bring out the best in followers, colleagues, and even other leaders.

Too many corporate CEOs have forgotten about meekness or humility. Check the photos and comments in business magazines and you'll know what we mean. They forget—on top of the world today, on the bottom tomorrow. Too many politicians have developed an air of detachment more akin to narcissistic celebrities than elected servants of the people. Check the news magazines and you'll see what we mean. Some politicians forget where they came from and whom they represent. Too many religious leaders have checked their meekness at the door of the church, dominating their parishioners like feudal lords. Check religious publications and websites and you'll find more than a few religious leaders who believe their own press.

Meek or humble leadership is not as contradictory as it sounds. Meekness is a matter of character and good leadership puts it into practice. Jesus said, "Whoever wants to become great among you must be your servant" (Matthew 20:26 and Mark 10:43). Both Moses and Billy Graham's leadership experiences serve as evidence that humility is, seemingly ironically, an ingredient of greatness.

"Until just recently," Danu said to them, "my

secretary named Esther, who loved people, she was

our actual leader.

She knew, really, about parking.

About exactly where to park.

In the faith lot.

That I didn't know until she left."

"Through Esther," Danu confessed,

"I learned the thing that we long for above all things . . . it

is love.

We all require love. The history of man is filled with our

Attempts to be great. Much of the world spends all of its

Time trying to be great, through war and through religious

activity, or in self works."

"Others try to bury their need for greatness in

material things.

In distractions. In working too much.

In entertainment.

In escape."

"Still others finally condemn themselves to despair and live out a sad, tormented, hopeless life, thinking greatness is reserved for only a few. Until recently I was living that hopeless life. Until Esther retired I couldn't quite put my finger on what was missing. What was wrong? Why greatness didn't feel great. To look at me you wouldn't have known I was hopeless. But I was. I also know three other people who have missed the only hope for greatness humankind has ever had. And peace. And joy. And meaning and significance.

Along with me, they couldn't stand at Esther's retirement because they had never allowed their hearts to be open to greatness.

To love and the freedom it brings.

Doing true greatness."

India is the cradle of Hinduism, Buddhism, Jainism, and Sikhism.

But Danu found, only upon his one day with Esther, that doing true greatness means accepting the Gospel of Jesus Christ.

And living for God,

using his talents, his wealth, his achievements for God's purposes.

And, ironically, at the end of his career

Danu learned some new rules for good living.

Shepherd Leaders

Our times are turbulent. Technology has given us a "think globally, act locally" public square that brings the world to our doorstep. It's a time that desperately needs leaders.

"Postmodernity" is the ten dollar word scholars use to describe our times. It's a term referencing the global culture that emerged in the late Twentieth Century and continues today. Actually, postmodernity is both a period of time and a belief system, both of which are characterized by "moral relativism" (a belief that truth cannot be defined or known, so neither can "right" or "wrong" be identified). It's also a time characterized by extroverted sensuality, consumer choice among an infinite variety of options—including spirituality—and a sense of "living in the now."

Postmodern men and women are able to do what's right in their own eyes. And "what's right" can literally be a construct of your own imagination. So one person's determination of "What's right" means nothing to the rest of us. We live in the now. We decide.

This sounds attractive in part because we're all "closet libertarians." We want to do what we want to do without interference. We want to follow our own self-generated rules for good living. We sing along with Sinatra, "I'll do it my way."

But this free wheeling emotional, social, economic, and political landscape is the very thing that causes people to feel uncertain, confused, anxious, and afraid. It's the cultural condition that creates people's hunger for leaders who can make sense of it all.

Religion doesn't seem to help much. Either religion has sold out to consumerism, offering schlock products rather than faith and wisdom for real life. Or religion is imploding on its own lack of confidence, no longer sure of its foundations or its vision for a better tomorrow. Of course if there is no truth, who cares what religion says anyway? As Bill Maher arrogantly claims, it's "religulous."

But therein is the problem. The idea that truth doesn't exist is a satanic lie. If we're deluded by this lie than maybe we'll forget that God is, that he is sovereign over world affairs, and that he has a plan for us.

For leaders or would-be leaders the "problem of our times" is also the "opportunity of our times." The more volatile the times, the more leaders can quickly make a difference. Like Roosevelt, who chose to address and alter the problems of his day, great leaders step up.

Postmodern times need leaders like Jesus, who— "When he saw the crowds, he had compassion on them, because they were harassed and helpless, like sheep without a shepherd" (Matthew 9:36). Our turbulent times need what might be called "shepherd leaders."

Shepherd leaders know all their sheep—their abilities, their needs, their unique challenges. Shepherd leaders know their environment and the threats within it. They know where they're going and why, and they know what their sheep need in order to do greatness.

Perhaps this analogy tends to break down, for not all followers are like sheep, nor are followers simply passive and leaders the absolute masters of their flocks. But there are still principles to glean in the idea of shepherd leaders.

Our postmodern times have deeply unsettled our culture, our country, and our colleagues, friends, and neighbors. Shepherd leaders with genuine Christian faith and hope, leaders who genuinely care about others, and leaders who genuinely give of themselves can bless their organizations and their communities with proactive perspective. These leaders do not depend upon religion but upon a relationship with Christ. These leaders know that their confidence and their competence come from the Lord. They believe in truth, so they speak truthfully. These leaders do greatness.

Danu,

a square man,

a leader, a follower,

a renewed man . . .

A heart following God.

A new man

a heart that not only feels right . . .

but is right.

Epitaphs

Eleanor Roosevelt has been called the most influential American woman of the Twentieth Century. This isn't her actual gravestone epitaph, but it's how she's remembered, so we might call it her practical epitaph. Will Rogers's memorial epitaph reads: "I never met a man I didn't like." It's one of Will's famous lines, capturing his spirit for those of us who never knew him.

Reclusive but influential poet Emily Dickinson's epitaph in Amherst, Massachusetts reads simply, "Called Back." The Temperance Movement reformer, Carrie Amelia Nation, who used a hatchet to attack saloons and wrote her name "Carry A Nation" for the publicity value, was laid to rest with this eloquent epitaph in Belton, Missouri: "She hath done what she could."

Old cemetery epitaphs are often thought-provoking and entertaining reading. A gravestone in Thurmont, Maryland says: "Here lies an atheist. All dressed up and no place to go." Or how about this one in Round Rock, Texas? "I told you I was sick."

One gravestone in New Mexico says, "Here lies the body of John Yeast. Pardon me for not rising." An epitaph in Winterborn Steepleton Cemetery, Dorsetshire, England reads, "Here lies the body of Margaret Bent. She kicked up her heels and away she went."

One of the most complimentary epitaphs you're ever likely to read is written upon the West Point gravestone of Lt. Col. Herbert Bainbridge Hayden. It reads: "In appreciation of a loyal friend, a square man, an efficient officer, in every way a thoroughbred.

The Bible also contains some wonderful epitaphs. Joshua's faithful leadership earned him this biblical comment. "Israel served the Lord throughout the lifetime of Joshua and of the elders who outlived him" (Joshua 24:31). At the time of his death John the Baptist was eulogized by Christ as, "among those born of women there has not risen anyone greater than John the Baptist" (Matthew 11:11).

In 2 Kings we read that King Hezekiah's pattern of life became his epitaph: "Hezekiah trusted in the Lord, the God of Israel. There was no one like him among all the kings of Judah, either before him or after him. He held fast to the Lord and did not cease to follow him; he kept the commands the Lord had given Moses. And the Lord was with him; he was successful in whatever he undertook" (18:5-7). Hezekiah lived a life worth living and he died a man honored for his service for the Lord.

Bad epitaphs are recorded in Scripture too. King Ahab and Queen Jezebel, along with their son Ahaziah are cited as the worst of the Old Testament royalty. And when you read the biography of Samson you think his epitaph must read, "What might have been!"

The Bible tells us Samson was the strongest man who ever lived. He accomplished incredible feats for God and his people Israel—killing lions with his bare hands, single-handedly defeating hundreds of his nation's enemies, and otherwise troubling Israel's belligerent neighbors until they were afraid to attack. Yet his strength and finally his life were taken from him because he allowed three women to lead him down an immoral path to destruction. While God forgave Samson and in the end restored his strength for one last heroic act against Israel's enemies, Samson's life and impact were cut short by his poor moral choices. What an epitaph he could have earned had he stayed focused upon the Lord.

What would any of us

have our headstones read:

"I followed Jesus, just like Danu . . ."

Your Epitaph

If you read the weekend obituaries in any local newspaper you'll see multiple columns entitled WWII Medalist, Austrian Playwright, Character Actor in 120 Films, Woman Who Wrote Beloved Nursery Rhymes, World's Richest Man, Screen Siren Dies at 92, Inventor, Mass Murderer, or Former Vice President Laid to Rest.

These are obituary headlines. In this postmodern age when it's no longer our custom to write about people's lives on their gravestones, these headlines serve as a type of epitaph. They summarize for us what the deceased accomplished in life and how they are likely to be remembered.

Epitaphs help us look beyond death to how quickly the world marches on, seemingly forgetting our time in the sun. Scripture says our lives are like "a mist that appears for a little while and then vanishes" (James 4:14). In more contemporary language some wiseacre once said that we quickly go from "Who's Who" to "Who's he?" or "Who's she?"

But the Bible tells us that no one lives to himself or even dies to himself. Whether we live or die we influence people around us and we belong to the Lord (Romans 14:7-8). One way of putting it is that while we'll not all become a "Who's Who" on the headline pages, in God's eyes we will never be "Who's he?" or "Who's she?"

Every day, we're influencing someone in a spiritually productive or unproductive way. Everyday our actions become reputations become legacies become epitaphs, the summary of our life and how we will be remembered—and what we carry into eternity.

The Apostle Paul left spiritual legacies wherever he traveled. In one of his letters, Paul points out to the believers in Corinth that they were the result of his ministry, "written not with ink but with the Spirit of the living God, not on tablets of stone but on tablets of human hearts" (2 Corinthians 3:3).

In other words, when Paul was in Corinth he lived for the Lord and led others to Jesus Christ. Then he taught them. When his ministry took him elsewhere Paul left behind Christian people as living letters—living legacies of his testimony for Christ. His epitaph was in some sense the people in whose lives he had invested.

What will your epitaph be? What will your associates write? What will God write?

Epitaphs don't just happen to us. They're crafted by our choices day by day, so in a very real sense we can write our own epitaph.

Remember Ebenezer Scrooge in "A Christmas Carol"? If you're reading this, it's not too late to start developing a better epitaph. Scrooge did.

How many headstones

Do you wonder about . . .

And if they could have ever been Re-

written,

Re-written to read the same—

"great and faithful servant"

To Whom Much Is Given

In the Gospel according to Luke, God reminds us, "From everyone who has been given much, much will be demanded; and from the one who has been entrusted with much, much more will be asked" (12:48).

To each of us has been given all that we need to live, to serve, to produce, and from each of us God will expect an accounting. He wants us to use our God-given gifts for good, that is, for His purposes and glory. Someday, the Scripture says, he will ask us what we did with our time, talent, and treasure (Hebrews 9:27).

Let's consider some of the things we've been given: 1) We live in a free country. For all its troubles, we live in one of the most opportunity-filled nations on earth. 2) We enjoy a biblically informed heritage in our culture. Despite the moral confusion we experience today, there is still an evident foundation of liberty based on law. 3) If you are a Christian, you possess a relationship with God in Heaven. You are blessed not only with political liberty but also with spiritual liberty in Christ. 4) We've each been given unique talents enabling us to care for our families, pursue our callings, develop culture, advance the cause of Christ in this world, and enjoy life.

We've been given a great deal; so much that it is difficult to comprehend it all. What then are we doing with all we've been given? And when we reach our golden years, will we look back with humble gratitude for what we've allowed God to do through us, or will we look back with regret?

Danu learned some new lessons in leadership.

And how leaders are shaped.

And he learned, finally, about doing greatness.

Jesus, The Truly Great

The greatest leaders excel not only at leadership but at "lifeship." They've learned how to live, so they're able to live out their values in and through their leadership experience.

The old question "Are leaders born or are they made?" is in one sense an amusing one. The answer is "Of course they are born; everyone is." But leadership skills can be learned—that is, leaders are "made." Leadership is crafted just as lifeship is crafted one decision at a time. Not all leaders who do greatness are born to it. They learn lessons of leadership that one day in God's providence find expression.

Jesus of Nazareth, for example, wasn't born in a log cabin or a mansion. He began his short time on earth in a manger or grotto near a Bethlehem inn with a "No Vacancy" sign on the door. His Mother, Mary, and her fiance, a man named Joseph whom she would later marry, were poor. Yet Jesus's conception was miraculous—the Son of the Living God born of a virgin—and angels heralded his birth. His first visitors, however, were shepherds, one of the more lowly jobs in the local agricultural economy.

Not much is recorded in Scripture about Jesus's youth except for a wonderful verse in Luke 2:52 stating, "Jesus grew in wisdom and stature and in favor with God and men." Jesus developed his human character in a manner that pleased God and blessed everyone who met him. He was, the Bible tells us, without sin, and when he turned 30 years of age he began his ministry according to the will of his Father in heaven.

We know that the Bible is not simply a leadership handbook, nor can Jesus's significance be limited to status as a leadership guru. Yet as the Savior and Lord in whom "we live and move and have our being," Jesus provides us with the greatest example of effective leadership we can ever identify (Acts 17:28). In three and one-half years Jesus led, taught, molded, and prayed for a motley crew of twelve disciples who he imbued with a faith so powerful it literally launched "The Way" that changed the world.

Jesus never led an organization. But he recruited and mentored followers, dealt with them fairly and truthfully, instilled core values, delegated responsibility for a mission, and empowered his followers so they could fulfill the mission. He used simple parables and word pictures, he spoke clearly and decisively, he revealed to his disciples his unique divinity as the Son of God, something they could not emulate, even as he demonstrated for them his humility as a man, something he commanded them to embrace and imitate.

Jesus personified and magnified love. He showed love, preached love, and lived a life of love. That love led him to a cruel death on the cross. Jesus so loved us that he gave himself for us and whoever believes in him will be saved from the power of sin in this life and the penalty of sin in eternity (John 3:16). If we accept Jesus Christ as our Savior, the Bible says God will forgive us our sins and make us one of his children (1 John 1:9).

Jesus led by example. He modeled a motive, content, and style of leadership that runs counter to human inclination and our current culture's lessons in leadership. In other words, current culture advises one approach to greatness in leadership, while Christian character demands another.

And then some . . .

a headstone on which

you

scroll

down . . .

there's more to the

story

Current Culture And Christian Character

Current culture teaches us that money is an end in itself. Christian character teaches us that money is not evil, that the pursuit of wealth rightly earned is not wrong, that possessing wealth is a gift of God to be used in his service, and that motive is ultimately more important than money.

Current culture over-emphasizes position, power, and prestige. Christian character considers position and power useful tools for developing worthy economic and cultural enterprises that support our families and benefit our communities. Christian character places position, power, and prestige in the service of virtues like love, truth, productive work, and honesty.

Current culture sometimes suggests people are peons, or worse, pawns, just rungs to be stepped upon while climbing the ladder of success. Christian character emphatically and profoundly states that every individual is made in the image of God and is loved by God. People intrinsically matter, and leaders who understand this build organizations that foster respect. Leaders who understand this avoid the pitfall of arrogance, for they know they cannot do it alone, and they do not even want to try.

Current culture says live for now. Christian character says live for eternity.

Current culture promotes fame and fortune as the ultimate measuring sticks of success. Christian character requires faith in God and good works based upon that faith, regardless of the calling we pursue.

Current culture smiles upon selfish ambition, but Christian character approves only of godly aspiration. Notice that Christian character does not proscribe ambition. The Creator God did indeed make us with a capacity to aspire, but our ambitions must be governed by godliness.

Current culture promulgates data, ever expanding knowledge as the best tool of the informed leader. Christian character respects knowledge and reason but always guides these resources with wisdom sourced in the Word of God.

Christian faith and the Christian worldview that springs from it call for a radically transformative understanding of life (Romans 12:1-2). Everything we do matters both now and for eternity because God created both us and the world in which we live. So the culture— way of life—we construct should be a spiritual act of worship toward God.

Current culture sells success as an end all, be all, that significance is something we earn for ourselves by good deeds, long after we've cared for our bank account. Christian character refuses to dichotomize success and significance, for whatever we do, whatever God allows us to achieve, we are to do it as unto the Lord. We don't work for success, than serve for significance. When we live a Christian philosophy of life, success and significance go hand in hand all along the way.

Our success and our significance are rooted together in relationship to God and his blessings.

And so Danu was determined to demonstrate the new rules

for good living and for leadership and for doing true

greatness . . . but first Danu felt he must return to

America,

one more time,

to talk with three people.

Though they supported his pursuit of greatness for over 30

years, serving him as loyal followers of company policy,

Danu needed to introduce them

to true greatness–the Gospel of true greatness—love.

True greatness, Danu said at 86,

lives not for the next investment return,

but for love's place in how you do greatness.

Danu was tired and sad,

for both his mother and father Godeep had died.

For all he learned from Godeep,

Danu felt he failed at teaching his father the most

important thing in the world–true greatness.

Only one of the three employees he met with responded to

how you do true greatness.

But Danu still writes the other two,

regularly,

just after he wakes each morning,

dresses,

drinks a glass of freshly-squeezed Florida orange juice,

looks into the bathroom mirror,

and states with conviction:

> "Today you do greatness . . . true greatness,
>
> through him . . . and by way of his love."

Today You Do Greatness

The Bible is full of examples of how God took ordinary, obedient people and empowered them with his spirit and vision to accomplish extraordinary things. The very best way to do greatness in the eyes of God is to apply biblical principles and values to first our lifeship and then our leadership. It's not about being great; it's about doing great for God. This is Jesus's model and his command.

"Today You Do Greatness" when you live and lead in a manner that allows the Lord to say, "Well done, good and faithful servant."

Sequential Topical Index

Acknowledgements

One of the lessons of greatness is that we cannot accomplish great things alone. That's certainly the case with this book. We, therefore, want to thank a panel of readers for their diligent, thought-provoking, and helpful comments on early drafts of *Today You Do Greatness.*

These friends include,

Bethany Carlson
Russell Carlson
Thomas Emigh
Doug Fagerstrom

Stan Jensen
David Murdoch
Roger Spoelman

Dr. Rogers's daughter, Elizabeth Rogers Drouillard, organized and set up the print version of this book.

In each instance their insights improved the final product, but errors in the text are ours alone.

About The Authors

Dr. Rick E. Amidon is Founder of mark217, a recovery ministry. He is former 23-year president of Baker College of Muskegon, Michigan and of Sanford-Brown College in Grand Rapids, Michigan. He serves on the faculty at the University of Phoenix and is the author of two books: *Jesus Trucking Company* (Halcyon Press, 2001) and *Spoken For* (Halycon Press, 2005). The inspiration for the story in *Today You Do Greatness* is based upon an Indian resident of a small rural community in mid-Michigan where Amidon grew up, a man who quietly emerged to lead a successful company to international "greatness." Dr. Amidon's new book, *Everything which Lives waits to be Noticed,* is scheduled to be published by Time-Warner early in 2012.

Dr. Rex M. Rogers is President of SAT-7 USA, www.sat7usa.org, the American arm of SAT-7, a Christian satellite television ministry broadcasting throughout the Middle East and North Africa. He is former 17-year president of Cornerstone University in Grand Rapids, Michigan and is the author of *Seducing America: Is Gambling A Good Bet?* (Baker, 1997), later revised and republished as *Gambling: Don't Bet On It* (Kregel, 2005). Dr. Rogers also authored *Christian Liberty: Living for God in a Changing Culture* (Baker, 2003) and an e-book, *Living For God In Changing Times* (2011). From 1993 to 2009, he was author and voice of "Making a Difference," a daily radio program applying a Christian worldview to current issues and events. In 2003 to 2008, the program was syndicated as a weekly column to more than 100 newspapers in 33 states. Beginning 2011, Missions in Media, Inc. produces "Making a Difference with Rex Rogers," a Christian commentary video column posted to www.relevantchristian.com and www.westmichiganchristian.com, for which Dr. Rogers also serves as Contributor, writing monthly articles.

His new book in development is *Be One of God's Unlikely Leaders—Live With Purpose, Get Things Done.*

Dr. Amidon wrote the fictional story in *Today You Do Greatness* while Dr. Rogers provided the commentary. Both authors speak regularly at churches, schools, commencements and other special events, business environments, and conferences.

Contact Dr. Amidon at dramidon@msn.com.

Read more of Dr. Rogers's writing at his blog, www.rexmrogers.com, follow him at www.twitter.com/RexMRogers or www.facebook.com/rexmrogers, or contact him at unlikelyleaders@gmail.com.

More About SAT-7

Satellite Television Transforming the Middle East Through HOPE in Jesus Christ

Founded in 1995, SAT-7, www.sat7.org, is a nonprofit Christian satellite television ministry broadcasting 24/7 across 22 countries in the Middle East and North Africa and 50 countries in Europe. Since its inception, Founder Dr. Terence Ascott, a British citizen who has lived in the Middle East for forty years, has served the ministry as International CEO.

The Middle East and North Africa is a region challenged by high levels of illiteracy, lack of opportunities for women, unemployment, and social unrest that in some countries turns to violence. While the Christian Church exists in the region, in various countries it is suppressed, may be pronounced illegal, and can be persecuted. Yet the Church is resilient and millions are open to Christ's love, forgiveness, hope, and the blessings of the Christian life.

SAT-7 broadcasts five channels in three languages: Arabic—SAT-7 ARABIC, SAT-7 KIDS, SAT-7 PLUS. Farsi (Persian)—SAT-7 PARS. Turkish— SAT-7 TURK.

A new sixth channel, SAT-7 NORTH AMERICA, was launched November 3, 2013 for Arabic language broadcasts throughout Canada, United States, Mexico, and Caribbean countries, www.sat7northamerica.org.

Based in Cyprus, the network maintains studios in Beirut, Lebanon; Cairo, Egypt; Istanbul, Turkey; Limassol, Cyprus; and London, England. About 80% of broadcast programming is produced in the Middle East by Middle Easterners.

SAT-7 is biblically Christian, nonpolitical and nonpartisan, culturally sensitive, and exists to encourage the Church and share the Gospel of Christ. The ministry is governed by the SAT-7 International Council, comprised of Christian leaders from the Middle East and North Africa, Europe, and North America.

SAT-7's viewership is conservatively documented at more than 15 million people with 9.25 million regularly watching SAT-7 KIDS. An independent media agency determined that an astounding 1 in 3 children in Iraq and 1 in 4 children in Saudi Arabia are watching SAT-7 KIDS.

"Seminary Of The Air" or SOTA is a Bible teaching series aired in Farsi on SAT-7 PARS. New Arabic language Bible teaching programs are being developed under the name "Theological Education for Arab Christians at Home" or TEACH. SAT-7 produces and airs music videos, dramas, films, game shows, worship services, discussion panels, cartoons, special events, and more.

While focused upon television broadcasting, SAT-7 is posting an ever-increasing amount of content on several network-developed YouTube channels and other social media outlets.

The ministry is supported by gifts via support offices in Europe, the UK, Canada, and the United States. SAT-7 USA's initiative to engage Western women with the spiritual and other needs of women and children in the Middle East and North Africa is called SAT-7 Women for Middle East HOPE, www.facebook.com/Sat7womenformiddleeasthope.

SAT-7 USA, P.O. Box 2770, Easton, MD, 21601, www.sat7usa.org, 866-744-7287.